THE POWER OF ONE QUESTION

Master the Art of Smart Questioning, Revolutionize Your Thinking & Decision-Making, Supercharge Your Life & Career and Ignite Your Journey to Greatness

Sooraj Achar

WWW.SOORAJ-ACHAR.COM

Copyright © 2023 by Sooraj Achar

All rights reserved.

No part of this book may be reproduced in any form without permission in writing from the author.

No part of this publication may be reproduced or transmitted in any form or by any means, mechanical or electronic, including photocopying or recording, or by any information storage and retrieval system, or transmitted by email or by any other means whatsoever without permission in writing from the author.

YOUR FREE GIFT

As a token of my thanks for taking out time to read my book, I would like to offer you a **Free-Gift**:

Scan the QR Code below to Download your **Free eBook PDF**.

Learn 395+ Surprising Psychology Words That Will Change The Way You Think - in the Next 30 Days!

You can also grab your **FREE GIFT** by typing in the below URL: **https://gift.sooraj-achar.com/**

ABOUT AUTHOR

Sooraj Achar, the Accomplished Author of **"The Power Of One Question"** - A Sensational **#1 Bestseller Across the Globe**

Dive into the world of **Sooraj Achar**, a prodigious author hailing from Bangalore, India, whose exceptional journey is as intriguing as the profound concepts explored in his works. With "The Fear of Death," Sooraj has transcended borders, achieving the coveted status of **#1 Bestseller** in the United States, the United Kingdom, Canada, India, and Australia.

A Remarkable Beginnings:

Sooraj Achar's extraordinary odyssey commenced in the vibrant city of Bangalore, India. As a young dreamer, his fascination with mathematics sparked an early connection with the enigmatic world of numbers. This infatuation, initially drawn from captivating numerological stories, sowed the seeds for a lifetime dedicated to the exploration of **Numerical Mysteries**.

A Multifaceted Expert:

Today, **Sooraj Achar** stands as not just an accomplished Software Engineer but also a passionate connoisseur of **numerology** and the ancient science of **Feng-Shui (Vastu)**. His multifaceted persona extends to **coaching and consulting**, where he delves into the profound questions of Health, Relationships, Careers, and Money (HRCM). Sooraj is a certified **Ho'oponopono & EFT Healer and NLP Practitioner**, renowned for his transformative abilities in bringing about balance, harmony, and fulfillment in the lives of countless individuals.

A Seeker of Wisdom:

Sooraj's relentless quest for knowledge has led him to the intricate realms of human psychology and behavior. His dedication to understanding the human psyche and optimizing life's potential is unwavering. As a perpetual learner, he embodies the principles of optimal living and shares his wisdom to empower others to lead resourceful lives.

A Believer in Unlimited Potential:

Above all, **Sooraj Achar** is a firm believer in the limitless potential residing within each individual. He ardently champions the idea that every person possesses the capacity to achieve far beyond their self-imposed limits. Through his words and wisdom, he inspires others to unlock their hidden potential and lead lives of purpose and abundance.

For more life-altering insights, delve into Sooraj Achar's remarkable catalog of books. Visit www.sooraj-achar.com and embark on a journey of self-discovery and transformation.

Stay Connected:

Explore the latest updates, thought-provoking content, and inspiring messages from Sooraj Achar by connecting with him through our social media channels. Join us in the pursuit of a fulfilling and harmonious life.

https://amzn.to/3CgQHF9

https://medium.com/@soorajachar99

https://bit.ly/3M7gIu2

instagram.com/psychology_of_numberz/

https://bit.ly/3dO6aDh

THE POWER OF ONE QUESTION

https://bit.ly/3LXBTyz

https://bit.ly/3E9vKxc

Acknowledgements

How does a person say "**Thank You**" when there are so many people to thank?

Obviously, this book is a big thank you to my father **G Sathyanarayan Achar,** who is a powerful role model, and to my mother **G Pramila,** who taught me love and kindness.

My dearest ones most responsible for this book becoming a reality is my sister **Shruthi S,** brother-in-law **Saravana P,** and my cute niece **Naveeksha S.** They make my life complete.

Special thanks to my Mentor **Mr. Mitesh Khatri**, who taught me and guided me to become a **Ho'Oponopono & EFT - Healer**.

I am grateful to **Mr. Som Bathla**, who is an Amazon **#1 Bestselling** author of multiple books; for mentoring, motivating, and guiding me to Write, Self-Publish, & Launch Books and for helping me start my **Authorpreneur Journey.**

Last but not least, My Team: **Avesh Ansari(Profile), Akshay Bhat(work4ever24h), & Md. Bilal (Iconic_agency).**

DEDICATION

This Book is Dedicated to My Grandparents,

R. Gangadharaiah & G. Vishalakshamma

And, My Dear Brother **Arvind Achar.**

CONTENTS

How This Book Can Work Miracles in Your Life? — XV

Chapter Highlights: Top 5 Takeaways & Insights — XXIII

1. The Question that Changes Everything — 1
2. Big Life Questions vs. Small Specific Questions — 10
3. Your Life, Your Questions: The Ultimate Transformation — 18
4. Developing Question Awareness for Personal Transformation — 22
5. Transforming Small Specific Questions — 27

6.	The Influence of Questions on Relationships and Interactions	35
7.	Big Life Questions and Their Influence on Your Life	42
8.	Mastering Big Life Questions	47
9.	Taking Control of Your Frequency	52
10.	The Art of Question Mastery for Self-Improvement	58

Conclusion	61
May I Ask You for a Small Favor?	63
Preview of My Best Selling Books	66
Testimonials	84
Author Profile	91
Disclaimer	94

How This Book Can Work Miracles In Your Life?

Introduction

In a world filled with constant noise, chaos, and an ever-growing thirst for knowledge, there exists a simple yet transformative tool that has the power to change your life – the art of asking one powerful question. This book, The Power Of One Question, is your guide to mastering the skill of smart questioning, revolutionizing your thinking and decision-making, supercharging your life and career, and igniting your journey to greatness. Are you ready to embark on this life-altering adventure?

Unveiling the Magic of One Question

Imagine having a magic wand that can unravel the most profound mysteries of your life, unlock hidden potentials, and guide you to a path of clarity and purpose. That magic wand is not fictional; it's the simple yet potent act of asking **one compelling question**.

The Power of a Single Question

The ancient Greek philosopher Socrates was known for his deep wisdom and understanding of the human mind. His method of questioning, referred to as the Socratic method, revolved around asking a series of carefully crafted questions to stimulate critical thinking and self-discovery. One of his fundamental beliefs was that "An unexamined life is not worth living."

In our journey through The Power Of One Question, we will delve into how a single question can spark self-reflection, foster innovation, empower decision-making, and transform your entire outlook on life.

1. Master the Art of Smart Questioning

The first step in the transformational journey that this book offers is mastering the art of smart questioning. Asking questions is an inherent human trait, but asking the right questions is a skill that can be developed and honed.

The Anatomy of a Smart Question

A smart question is a key that unlocks doors to knowledge, understanding, and solutions. It is framed to target the heart of an issue, encouraging thoughtful responses and introspection. Learning to craft smart questions is like wielding a master key that can open countless doors in your life.

In The Power Of One Question, we will dissect the elements of a smart question, explore various question types, and provide practical exercises to help you create your own powerful inquiries. With this skill, you will be equipped to navigate the intricate terrain of your mind and the world around you.

2. Revolutionize Your Thinking

The journey to greatness begins with a shift in your thought patterns. This transformation requires an exploration of your current beliefs, assumptions, and mental paradigms.

Breaking Free from Conventional Thinking

Conventional thinking is a product of habit, routine, and conformity to societal norms. It limits our potential, stifles creativity, and hinders progress. To ignite your journey to greatness, you must liberate yourself from these mental constraints.

The Power Of One Question introduces techniques to break free from conventional thinking. We explore real-life examples of individuals who defied the norm and created revolutionary change. By shifting your mindset from conformity to curiosity, you will gain the ability to challenge the status quo and embrace innovation.

3. Empower Your Decision-Making

Our lives are defined by the choices we make. The decisions we face may range from the mundane to the life-altering, and our ability to make informed and confident choices can impact our future profoundly.

The Decision-Making Toolkit

Every decision is an opportunity to shape your destiny. However, making decisions can be a daunting task, often clouded by uncertainty and fear of making the wrong choice. In The Power Of One Question, we provide you with a decision-making toolkit that equips you to handle choices of all magnitudes.

Learn how to evaluate your options, align your decisions with your values and aspirations, and gain the courage to act upon them. The art of smart questioning will illuminate the path ahead, making you an adept decision-maker in your personal and professional life.

4. Supercharge Your Life & Career

With the art of smart questioning, you hold the key to supercharging every aspect of your life and career. From personal growth to professional success, this book guides you on a journey toward a life of fulfillment and accomplishment.

Aligning Goals with Smart Questions

Do you seek personal growth, better relationships, or career advancement? The Power Of One Question empowers you to align your goals with the art of smart questioning. When your aspirations are paired with the ability to ask insightful questions, the sky is the limit.

Supercharge your personal growth by examining your life's purpose, nurture meaningful relationships by seeking profound understanding, and elevate your career by making strategic decisions. This transformational guide offers you the tools to design your destiny.

5. Ignite Your Journey to Greatness

Greatness is not a destination; it's a journey. This journey is illuminated by the art of smart questioning. *The Power Of One Question* empowers you to initiate your quest for greatness, where every question becomes a stepping stone towards your extraordinary future.

Achieving Miracles in Your Life

The word "miracle" is often associated with divine intervention, but in truth, miracles are often the result of profound self-discovery, conscious decisions, and the magic of asking one powerful question.

By immersing yourself in the art of smart questioning, you will unlock the miracles that lie within your grasp. The mundane will transform into the extraordinary, insights will guide you, and opportunities will abound. Your journey to greatness starts with a single question and the commitment to self-improvement.

Conclusion

The Power Of One Question is more than a book; it's a transformative journey. Whether you are on a quest for personal growth, seeking a path to professional success, or simply curious about the art of smart questioning, this guide will equip you with the tools you need to supercharge your life.

So, are you ready to embark on this remarkable journey? The power of one question awaits, and with it, the potential to unlock miracles in your life, revolutionize your thinking, and ignite your journey to greatness. Your adventure begins now, with the turn of the first page."

CHAPTER HIGHLIGHTS: TOP 5 TAKEAWAYS & INSIGHTS

1. Key Takeaways for the Chapter: The Question that Changes Everything

1. Change Happens in an Instant: The chapter highlights how success and failure can occur in a split second, emphasizing that even the smallest adjustments can have a profound impact on your life's trajectory.

2. Minute Differences Lead to Significant Outcomes: Examples, such as the subtle

variations in facial expressions or the angle of a cricket bat, illustrate how tiny differences in actions or thoughts can result in contrasting results.

3. The Power of One Decision: The chapter underscores the significance of individual decisions, stating that a single choice can dramatically alter the course of one's life, affecting destiny and destination.

4. Quality of Questions Shapes Your Life: Questions play a pivotal role in shaping your thoughts, emotions, and ultimately your actions. The chapter suggests that understanding and controlling the questions you ask yourself can significantly impact your life's quality.

5. The Question-Answer Thought Process: The thinking process is described as a continuous loop of questions and answers within your mind. It is emphasized that controlling the quality and nature of your

self-directed questions can influence the direction of your thoughts and feelings.

2. Key Takeaways for the Chapter: Big Life Questions Vs. Small Specific Questions

1. Big Life Questions: These questions have a profound impact on various aspects of your life, affecting health, relationships, careers, and money. Examples include "Why is my life like this?" or "Why am I struggling?" Becoming aware of these questions and their effects on your life can be transformative.

2. Small Specific Questions: These are specific, situational questions that may be negative or positive in nature. They can impact your emotions and actions. For instance, asking, "If I don't have intimacy in my marriage, what's the point of being married?" negatively influenced one's feelings and relationships. Choosing the right specific questions can lead to positive changes.

3. The Power of Small Questions: Small questions, even if they appear situation-specific, can significantly impact your emotions and life. The example of a coach's question about improving conversions highlights the importance of framing small questions positively to boost motivation.

4. Emotional Impact: The questions you ask yourself can affect your emotions. Negative questions tend to create dissatisfaction, frustration, and negative feelings, while positive questions can enhance motivation and positivity.

5. Self-Reflection: The chapter encourages self-awareness about the questions you repeatedly ask yourself, as these questions can have far-reaching effects on your life and mindset. Recognizing and altering these questions can lead to positive change.

3. Key Takeaways for the Chapter: The Transformational Role of Questions

1. Unconscious Questions: The questions you unconsciously ask yourself, such as "When will I lose

weight?" after exercising and checking your weight daily, can affect your emotions and actions. These questions may lead to motivation or demotivation based on their nature.

2. Impact on Relationships: Negative questions, like those about in-laws or life partners not understanding or listening, can lead to negativity and issues in relationships. Becoming aware of the impact of such questions is essential for improving relationships.

3. Direction of Life: Small questions, even seemingly insignificant ones, can gradually change the course of your life. Over time, they can lead to a completely different destination and destiny. Recognizing this can help you make conscious changes in your life.

4. Question-Driven Beliefs: The questions you ask can shape your beliefs and emotional frequencies. It's essential to choose questions that motivate and support your goals rather than hinder them.

5. Positive Changes: Changing the questions you ask yourself can lead to positive outcomes and emotional shifts. By consciously selecting questions that empower you, you can influence your actions and overall well-being.

4. Key Takeaways for the Chapter: Developing Question Awareness for Personal Transformation

1. Small Changes, Big Impact: Small changes in your direction, angle, or positioning can lead to significant differences in outcomes. Just like adjusting an airplane's course by ten degrees can result in a completely different landing destination.

2. Cricket Bat Analogy: Playing the same shot in cricket with a minute difference in the angle of the bat can lead to a completely different result. Even slight variations can make a substantial impact.

3. Daily Application: Implementing this concept in your daily life can have a profound effect, taking

you to new heights. Embracing small techniques can lead to substantial life improvements.

4. The Power of Questions: Our brains are wired with neurons that function as questions. The thinking process is essentially a series of questions and answers. The quality of questions determines your thought quality, leading to positive or negative thoughts.

5. Quality of Questions and Life: The quality of your questions directly influences your frequency, which, in turn, shapes the quality of life you attract. To control your attractions, focus on controlling your questions, which control your frequency. Small specific questions pertain to specific situations, areas of life, or individuals..

5. Key Takeaways for the Chapter: Transforming Small Specific Questions

1. Small Specific Questions Shape Your Frequency: Small specific questions influence your frequency

and ultimately shape your thoughts and emotions in various aspects of your life.

2. Empowering Questions: Replace negative questions with empowering ones to change your thought patterns and emotional states. For example, shift from "Why am I not losing weight?" to "Why am I motivated to exercise every day?"

3. Improve Clarity and Power: By altering the questions you ask yourself, you can improve clarity and generate a sense of power, even if you don't currently feel that way. For instance, ask, "Why am I so clear in life?" or "I don't know why I am so powerful?"

4. Career and Promotion Questions: Change disempowering career-related questions like "Why am I not getting a promotion?" to empowering ones like "Why do I always get everything so effortlessly?"

5. Money and Abundance Questions: Transform questions about money and wealth, such as "When will I make money?" to more positive ones like "Why do I always have the exact amount of money I need?"

or "Why am I attracting such big opportunities?" to feel blessed and attract abundance.

6. Key Takeaways for the Chapter: The Influence of Questions on Relationships and Interactions

1. Identify Negative Questions: Recognize and jot down the negative, small specific questions you've been asking yourself regarding your health, relationships, career, and money. Awareness of these negative questions is crucial.

2. Change Your Questions: Shift from negative questions to positive ones to influence your own thoughts and the responses you receive from others.

3. Transmit Positivity: Remember that what you transmit to people is what you attract from them. Transmit positive questions to receive positive responses.

4. Practice Seeding: Use questioning as a powerful way to seed positive ideas and affirmations in the minds of your children, loved ones, and yourself.

Encourage positivity with questions like, "Why do you remember things so easily?"

5. Make Questions Easier: Adding "I don't know why" at the beginning of your questions can make them more effective, especially in your subconscious mind. Transform negative questions into positive ones and practice this regularly to change your frequency and attract positive experiences.

7. Key Takeaways for the Chapter: Big Life Questions and Their Influence on Your Life

1. Big Life Questions: Big life questions are inquiries that have a significant impact on all areas of your life (HRCM - Health, Relationships, Career, Money). Questions like, "Why am I not confident?" or "What's the point?" are examples of such questions.

2. Danger of "What's the Point?": Asking, "What's the point?" can diminish your life experiences and motivation, leading to self-sabotage and missed opportunities.

3. Self-Destructive Patterns: When you have a low frequency due to negative big life questions, you may sabotage your own success, miss out on opportunities, and create a negative loop.

4. Changing Your Frequency: Recognize and transform your big life questions to boost your frequency and attract more positive experiences in your life.

5. Multiple Big Life Questions: You may have more than one big life question, and it can significantly affect your overall well-being. Identifying and changing these questions is essential for personal growth and success.

8. Key Takeaways for the Chapter: Mastering Big Life Questions

1. Identifying Big Life Questions: Big life questions are those that impact all areas of your life, leading to negative emotions. Examples include questions like, "Why do I always get things with so much struggle?" or "Why am I stuck?"

2. Effects of Negative Questions: These big life questions can result in depression, panic attacks, self-doubt, low self-esteem, and an inferiority complex, all contributing to low frequencies.

3. Changing Negative Questions: Transform these negative questions into positive alternatives. For instance, change "Why am I always so guilty?" to "How come I always find people who support me?"

4. Practice Over Questions: While asking questions is useful, real change comes from practice, not just questioning. Focusing on positive questions is more effective in improving your frequency and life experiences.

5. Taking Control: Understand that the questions you ask yourself have a significant impact on your life. By changing negative questions to positive ones, you can regain control of your thoughts, emotions, and overall frequency.

9. Key Takeaways for the Chapter: Taking Control of Your Frequency

1. Recognizing Subconscious Programming: People around you may unconsciously ask negative questions, influencing your subconscious mind. Instead of reacting negatively, respond with positive questions that can uplift both you and the other person.

2. Majority Frequency Dominance: We all possess positive and negative frequencies, and the one with the majority will dominate the other. If you focus on increasing your positivity, you can impact and uplift those with more negative frequencies.

3. Transforming Toxicity with Positivity: Like the story of Valmiki, you have the power to transform negativity into positivity. Don't ask how to handle negative people, but rather, ask how to become more positive.

4. Conflict Management: When facing conflict or anger, ask empowering questions like, "Why am I so

good at influencing people?" or "Why am I so good at negotiations?" This mindset shift can help you handle conflicts more effectively.

5. Embrace Responsibility: Instead of questioning "Why me?" when given more responsibility, think, "Why not me?" Recognize the opportunity for personal growth and development in handling increased responsibilities.

10. Key Takeaways for the Chapter: The Art of Question Mastery for Self-Improvement

1. Assignment Number One - Recognize and Transform Questions: Identify and differentiate your negative big life questions and small specific questions. Categorizing them is helpful but not mandatory. The crucial part is recognizing these negative questions and then transforming them into positive and powerful questions.

2. Assignment Number Two - Compare Old and New Questions: Compare your old negative

questions with the newly formulated positive ones. This comparison activates your subconscious mind, indicating your intention to change, improve, and grow.

3. Assignment Number Three - Loudly Repeat Positive Questions: Vocalize your positive questions aloud, not just in your mind. Stand in front of a mirror to observe your transformation, energization, and the positive impact on yourself and your surroundings. Repeat these questions multiple times a day to experience the changes taking place in your life.

These assignments are vital for effectively shifting your mindset and experiencing positive changes.

CHAPTER 1

THE QUESTION THAT CHANGES EVERYTHING

"The power of one question can alter the course of your life and lead you to greatness." – Sooraj Achar

A World of Change in a Split Second

This chapter is all about learning. How do you create more results in very less time in your life? What do you think is the amount of time that somebody can take to go from failure to success?

You may be thinking about a long period of time but actually, it just takes a second. Actually, the difference between success and failure is just this much. It takes 1 second to go from success to failure and from failure to success, both ways. How? Let me give you an example.

Make a serious face first, now make a happy face, now make a bored face, and then make an exciting face, now a confident face, and now a lazy face. Can you tell what was the difference in your body language in terms of measurement between a positive emotion and a negative emotion? Was it like a one-foot difference in your face? I mean, you don't even have that big face. But how much was the difference if you had to measure with a scale? How much was the difference in your expressions between sadness and happiness? If you were sad versus you were happy, how much was the difference? If you were lazy versus you were confident, how much was the difference in your facial expressions? Was it like half a foot, six inches? No, it is just like maybe just half an inch. When you smile and when you show a sad face it's just one inch difference.

So there are techniques which if you learn properly, you can understand that the difference between success and failure is just this much.

Let me give you one more example. You may have played cricket or you've enjoyed watching cricket. Suppose a bowler is throwing a ball at you, to hit a six you have to plan before the delivery that you want to hit the six on this ball, so you swing your bat with the intention of hitting the six. And you can make the ball travel outside the boundary. Now it's time for the second delivery, the bowler is throwing the ball towards you, now you hit with the same intention, the same strategy, and everything's the same. Is it possible that in the second ball, instead of getting a six, you can be out on the stump? Yes, it's possible. You may have seen this happening on the cricket ground, on the match, on TV. When the player is playing the same shot. The bowler is bowling the same, everything is the same, why are the results different? The first time he gets a six whereas the second time the batsman gets out on the stumps. What is the measurement difference? Most probably it's the angle of the bat. In the second attempt, the angle of the bat was slightly different, it wasn't huge but the difference of a few degrees made the player out. If we talk in Inches it was not even one inch. Sometimes it's literally 2 mm. Have you ever seen a match where when the guy gets out, they have to call for a third umpire because the umpire is confused about whether the ball touches the bat or not? Have you ever seen that situation in a match that goes to a third umpire? Nowadays there is sophisticated material, sophisticated cameras, and microphones that are installed near the stump. So what they do is in the camera, in the third umpire checks by reversing and playing the footage. And look for that slight sound when the ball touches the bat. And if they can find that the sound was there, it's out. The difference between hitting a six and getting out is not even one inch. It's just 1 mm. It's difficult to even calculate. You got my point. They have to literally take a computer and calculate by listening to the sounds and the visuals again and again and again.

So I just wanted to explain that the difference between success and failure is very small. If you make that one small change in your frequency, your life, instead of going here, will go there. One last example. Let's say you're going by flight, flying at 10,000ft. What is the speed at which a normal flight is running? The cars that we drive run at about 120 max. These flights can go up to 500 km/hour. But if it's an international Boeing, It can go up to 800-900 km/hour. So the point is that a flight is running at full speed. Now, is the flight following a particular angle in order to reach the destination? Yes. Now, if I change the angle of the flight by just two degrees on the left for half an hour, it will completely change the destination of the flight. Instead of Pune, you can land in Mumbai. If you just change that two degrees for half an hour running at 500 km, it can go in a completely different direction. Our life is like this. You make one small change in your life and your life directions can change.

Let me give you one last example here. Did this happen to you- you took one decision and that changed the direction of your life completely. Have there been some powerful decisions in your life? Either positive decisions or negative, that doesn't matter, But have you made some decisions that if you had not taken that decision today your life would have not been the same? Not one, there have been multiple such decisions in your life. And that one decision has changed the destiny of your life. And today, the destination of your life has changed because of that one decision. For example, if you were not married to the person with whom you're with right now you would have married to somebody else. That one small decision would have changed the course of your life. Would have changed the destiny of your life.

We can go in different directions in life. Just one single decision can change everything. So let's understand that one small technique can make big changes in your life in just one small shift in your frequency. What is that technique? It's a beautiful technique called questions. What do I mean by questions? Let me show you this. The quality of your questions controls the quality of your life. Now there are two types of questions. But before that, let me clarify something to you. What do you think- our frequency is inside us or outside us? It's inside. What is your frequency made of? Do you have wires inside you? Do you have plugs inside you? Do you have buttons inside you? No.

I've shown you so many ways to change your feelings. But many times your feelings are controlled by your thoughts. And many times when you start thinking negatively you just can't control it. It's like a slippery slope where if you start, you're not able to stop. And then those negative thoughts become negative emotions. Those negative emotions become strong and they become negative beliefs. And these negative beliefs become negative actions. And then we either do things in life that take us in a completely wrong direction or we don't do things in life which take us in the wrong direction.

Our thoughts are very powerful. So how do you control these thoughts? The best way to control your thoughts is to understand what the process of thinking is. The process of thinking is question and answer. Every time you're thinking in your mind, you're not aware of this but you're always doing a Q and A in your mind. For example, do you notice some questions that you ask yourself during the day which become your thoughts? The answers are always readymade. And who gives you the answers? You yourself. Because you're asking the question to yourself. So it's always you giving yourself the answer. So if you ask yourself a negative question by default, by default you will get an answer from your subconscious mind and it will always be a negative answer. Unfortunately, most of us are not able to control our thinking because we don't control the questions that we ask ourselves. Because these questions are running on autopilot. We are blind about it. We don't even know that we are working with questions and answers in our minds. But if you think about it slowly, the entire thinking process is nothing but a question-answer format in our brains.

There may be questions in your mind about your life, like What is going on in your life? Is this how my life should be? Why do I deserve this? Do I deserve this? Why me? Why am I going through this? Why am I suffering so much? What the hell? When will I recover this in my life? Why do I have to be so dependent on my wife? Why can't I do things on my own? Why is my life like this? Will I ever recover? These are negative kinds of questions. And these questions are happening at the speed of 500 in our brains. We don't even know they're happening. The question happens. Thought happens, feeling happens. Why is my life like this? And that's it. We go into a negative emotion after that.

Chapter 2

BIG LIFE QUESTIONS VS. SMALL SPECIFIC QUESTIONS

"The strength of your destiny lies in the questions you ask, not the answers you receive." – Sooraj Achar

Big Life Questions: Shaping Your Destiny

So how can you change your thoughts before even the negative thought comes? Start controlling the quality of your questions. If you change the quality of your questions consciously, you change the quality of your life. So I'll make it very, very simple for you. There are two kinds of questions that you have in your life, that you are always asking yourself. To make it very easy, I've kept the words very simple this time and kept it very, very easy for you.

The first kinds of questions are big life questions. Now what are big life questions? Big life questions are questions which give you impact your entire life situation. Everyone, quickly show me with your hands. A big question will give you an answer and an impact on this situation or almost every situation of life. That's why it's called not a small question. It's called a big question. And it's not called a situational question. It's called a life question.

Why is my life like this? Is this a small question or is this a big life question? Big life question. Why am I like this? What kind of question is this? It's a big life question. And it impacts not your small area of life; it impacts your entire life. This means it impacts all four areas of life: Health, relationships, career, and money. Why am I struggling in my life? It's a big life question. You keep asking this question again and again, your entire life gets screwed up. And most of us don't even know that we are asking these big life questions to ourselves.

I'll give you an example of myself. I had one big particular life question. And can you have more than big life questions? Sure. There can be one or two really big ones which you kind of repeat every time like a pattern in your life. So I'll tell you one of my patterns, one of my habits which I realized when I learned about a big life question in my life. Many years ago, I was very, very lazy in life. But I had this one weird pattern. I would get motivated sometimes; and get super excited to do something in my life. I would start taking action. For example, I would start exercising. And after two or three days of exercising, I will ask myself this question. What's the point of doing this? What do you think happened to my emotion of motivation? I started thinking that there's no point doing it, forget it. And I would go back to my old habits. My old patterns will come back and my old attraction will come back. You may have experienced something like this in your life. So your big questions in one instant can reverse everything you've done for the last ten days, ten months, one year.

I would go for a holiday and before going for the holiday, I was super excited. My thoughts were I'll do this and I'll do this and I'll do that. Waiting for the holiday. And once I reached the day after a few hours not even a few days after a few hours like two to 3 hours of reaching there guess what question I would ask myself? What's the point? What's the point of this holiday? What did I get doing all the fun? Can you see how easily I screwed up my holiday? And for the next three, or four days, while I was on that holiday, I was roaming around thinking, what's the point? And then maybe I'll get excited about something else.

One question destroys what? One smile destroys everything. One degree to the left and right takes the flight to another level. One angle difference in the bat and the person is out instead of a sixer. This is how powerful your questions are. But we don't even realize that we have some of these big questions.

Small Specific Questions: Unraveling Everyday Challenges

Now let's talk about the second kind of questions. The second kind of questions are called small specific questions. These are not big questions, but they are very specific. They're very small. And what will they impact? Will they impact now or will they impact forever?

Let's take an example. So, I had this very bad habit of whenever I was talking to my wife I would ask a stupid question about my relationship. If I don't have intimacy in my marriage then what's the point of being married? This one question was a small question. It was only and only related to my marriage. And it was only related to one situation in my marriage. But was this a positive question or a negative question? And how was it making me feel? It's a negative type of question and it was making me feel like I'm deprived of things in life.

I would feel depressed, I would feel frustrated, and I would feel bad, I would feel lonely; I used to feel hurt like I was not good enough. Like, why am I this one thing and not there in my life? Like, why am I not good enough? The point is, it was destroying my relationship. And this one question, believe it or not, the first two years of my marriage, subconsciously, I was repeating and repeating and repeating and repeating. It was just going on and on and on and on and on. Can you imagine the impact of this question? If I'm repeating that question almost 24 hours a day, it must be creating havoc inside me.

You're going through a storm inside you sometimes. The storm is created by a small thing. Either it's your big question or it's your small question. There is one particular coach whom I know because I am in a group of coaches where I'm also learning with some coaches. This one particular coach, every time his webinar is completed, asks this question: why are my conversions not improving? Is this a big life question or a small specific question? Yeah! It's a small, very situational, and only webinar-related question, but a positive question or a negative question? It's a positive one because it motivates him to make more conversions. If you were this coach all the time, how would you feel? You finished a webinar, you made one lakh rupees, I'm not kidding, I'm talking about somebody who finishes a one-hour webinar and makes one lakh. This person makes one lakh in 1 hour and says, when will my webinars increase my conversions? When will they increase? Immediately after the webinar, he looks at the number conversion and oh, when will my webinar conversions increase? And guess how he feels? He feels miserable. He feels unsatisfied. He feels disappointed. With whom? With himself. He feels he's not giving his best. Do you think with this kind of frequency he's going to grow in his coaching business? Absolutely yes.

And then there's another girl I know. She always asks this question: why is my income not higher than last month? And the number I'm talking to you was nine lakhs last month. And this month is eight lakhs. I'm not joking. Last month it was nine lakhs. And this month is eight lakhs. The question she's asking is why is my income not higher than last month? Guess, how is she feeling? She's made eight lakhs this month but what is the feeling she has with this question? She's actually feeling a lack of money, she's feeling like a failure, she's feeling miserable, she's actually feeling sad and she's feeling like there's something wrong with her. And she's constantly feeling bad. And she's desperate like, why is my income not higher than last month? Is this a great question to ask about this situation? No, it's a stupid question because she doesn't need that much money for her expenses; she can live a luxurious life with that money. So there is no point in expecting more money.

Chapter 3

Your Life, Your Questions: The Ultimate Transformation

"Never underestimate the influence of a well-timed, powerful question; it can change your life." — Sooraj Achar

How Questions Control Your Thoughts

Here's another question. You're exercising and you're asking this question: when will I lose weight? So every day you exercise, you get onto the scale. You may have made a stupid mistake. One day you exercise and look at the scale. On the second day you exercise and look at the scale. It's so stupid. And then you go through that same stupid emotion again. Think, will you feel motivated or demotivated to exercise the next day? That's why you give up. It controls your emotions. It controls your actions.

So now that you've understood the impact of these questions, I hope you are realizing that you are asking these questions unconsciously. You're not even doing it consciously. Like, many married people have this question about their mother-in-law: Why does my mother-in-law not accept me? Why doesn't she understand me? Why doesn't she respect me? Many people have questions with their life partner like: Why doesn't he/she listen to me? Why don't you listen to me? And you even say it on your life partner's face like, why don't you listen to me? The more you ask, the more you'll attract negativity from your partner because all these are negative questions.

The Small Questions That Shape Your Everyday Reality

One small question can change the direction of your life. And if you change the direction today, it may seem like a small direction change. But if you walk in that direction one more day and one more day and one more day and two more years and three more years and ten more years, you will have a totally different destination, a totally different destiny. You can relate that two years ago, three years ago you made some decisions that got you where you are today.

One last example: I was talking to a friend of mine, he's a coach himself and I suggested he start writing books. And he said, Sooraj, I can't achieve what you're achieving. I said why? Why'd you say that? He said, Sooraj, you've been writing books for the last two years. I said yes. He said, if you calculate that's 365 multiplied by two that's almost 700 days you are writing. I said okay. So he said, that means every day you've written at least one page.

He actually went on my Author Profile and did the calculation and he said, you've got more than 8 books. Then he said, when will I achieve what you have achieved? The moment he asked me that question he was talking to me. But my brain is tuned to listening to these frequency-related things like beliefs and emotional frequencies and patterns and all of this and suddenly I get this question of his. Is this the first question, the big life question? Or is this the second question, the small life but specific question? It's the Second one. But do you think it motivates him to write books? No, it doesn't. And does he sleep peacefully when he thinks about me? No, he doesn't. I asked him, I said, just change this question and see what happens. I'll tell you about that later.

Chapter 4

Developing Question Awareness for Personal Transformation

"Your life's narrative is written one question at a time, so make each one count." — Sooraj Achar

In this chapter, we are going to learn about what's the one thing that can make a major difference in your frequency. For example, let's say you change the direction of the flight which you're flying from only by ten degrees. But an airplane flies at a very, very high speed. Now, if you change the direction of the flight only by ten degrees and it keeps traveling at that ten degrees left or right from its original direction at full speed, after 3 hours, where will the flight land? The direction where you wanted to go or somewhere else? Yes! It will land somewhere else. But the change started with how many degrees? With just ten degrees. With a degree change, if you keep going and going, it goes in a completely different direction.

Another example, let's say you're playing cricket. Imagine I'm throwing a ball at you. I want you to hit a sixer. I threw the ball, you moved your bat and the ball touched the boundary, and you got a six. I'm going to throw the same ball in the same style, the same bowler, nothing is going to change. I want you to hit the same shot again. Now this time instead of getting a six, is it possible your wicket can be out? It's possible. You were playing the same shot but this time your bat was slightly shifted from the previous position. What is the difference between the angle of the bat and spacing? Is it like a one-foot angle difference or 2 ft angle difference? No. it was a couple of mm sometimes. And the ball can just touch the bat and go and hit the wicket. Which means a small difference can make a big difference.

If you apply this lesson every day in your life, it's a small technique but it will make a huge impact in your life and take you to a completely different level.

Another example: sit in a confident position, feel confident, and observe your body language, now sit in a low confidence position and again observe your body language. How much is the angle difference in your body language? Is it like a huge angle difference? You may have observed a very low difference between both positions. But that one small difference can be the difference between huge confidence frequency to low confidence frequency.

There's a lesson that I've learned from NLP. NLP is Neuro-linguistic psychology. I will discuss this later through a different book. NLP gives us the power to understand that our brain is made of neurons. And these neurons are nothing but questions. So every time you ask a question your brain is how the thinking process happens. Thinking is a process of questions and answers. Unconsciously, we are always asking ourselves questions. And the quality of questions you ask is the quality of frequency you have. Why? Because the quality of questions you have is the quality of answers you get.

Now, all the answers are nothing but thoughts. What are the two kinds of thoughts in the world? Positive thoughts and negative thoughts. Simple as that. So, if you ask positive questions, what kind of answers do you get? Positive thoughts. So what would you call that frequency? Positive frequency. That is why I said the quality of questions you ask is the quality of frequency you have. And the quality of frequency you have is the quality of life you attract. So, the quality of questions, quality of frequency, quality of life, and attraction all are connected to each other.

If I want to control my attractions, I don't even need to control my thoughts. I need to control only one thing. That is "questions". If you control your questions, you control your frequency.

Now, there are two types of questions. First are small specific questions. Small specific questions are situation-related and people-related. They are related to four areas of life: health, relationships, career, and money. Some questions are only related to health. Some questions are only related to relationships. Some questions are only related to career. And some questions are only related to money. Some questions are related to one particular person. So whenever you're asking a question that relates to only one specific situation one specific area or one specific person, it's called a small specific question.

Chapter 5

TRANSFORMING SMALL SPECIFIC QUESTIONS

"The journey to greatness starts with the courage to ask 'Why?' just once." — Sooraj Achar

A small specific question creates your frequency. Now, let's take an example. What is the color of the curtains of your room? It's a small specific question. Just like this, we have small specific questions related to our HRCN. I'll give you one area, one question. Example: in your health, you're asking, why am I not losing weight? Now the more you ask, why am I not losing weight? Are you motivated to exercise? No! Now if you change your question, you change your thoughts. You change your quality of frequency. Example: let's change the question from Why am I not losing weight to something else. Let's create a positive question out of it. Why am I motivated to exercise every day? I don't know why. Now check how that makes you feel. Just by asking questions like 'I don't know why', I feel like exercising all the time. I don't know why I'm always motivated to exercise. Now it gives you that feeling of oh wow! You feel powerful. You feel active. You feel lovely, you feel happy, and you feel energetic. If you ask an energetic question to your mind, you get an energetic thought. A lot of people say, how do I stop overthinking? You change your questions because thinking is a result of questions. Example: why does my father never listen to me? If you keep asking that same question again, again and again, and again and again, you're going to overthink all that. But if you simply ask, why is my father so nice to me all the time? Say this question loudly and check what thoughts come to you. Suddenly you will start getting good memories of your father being nice to you. So change your questions, change your life. Be aware of the negative questions that you're asking yourself, small specific negative questions for health, relationship, career, and money, and change them.

Here's a small specific question about yourself "Why am I so lazy?" How do you feel when you ask this question? You feel lazier. You feel more demotivated and not good. Ask yourself this question: why am I so clear in life? Just ask that question to yourself. See what happens. Why am I so clear in life? And now tell me how you feel. Yeah. You suddenly feel clarity. You see, you feel powerful. Repeat: "I don't know why I am so powerful?" Check how you feel, you actually feel good. Now some people will say, but I'm not powerful. But that's the point. You want to create power, right? You don't want to wait for power, you want to create power. See magicians create ordinary people to wait. Remember that magicians create ordinary people wait. Are you going to wait or are you going to create? If you're going to create, I'm showing you a technique of how to create. Change your questions; change your creation from negative to positive. If you want to change your thinking, change the questions.

I'll give you career examples: Why am I not getting a promotion? See how you feel. You feel sad, you feel stressed, and you feel confused like I don't know what to do. Now change that question and repeat loudly "Why do I always get everything so effortlessly? " "I don't know why?" How do you feel now? Just changing that question, how did you feel? It suddenly makes you feel good in one instant. Why? Because you're changing your questions you're changing your thoughts, you're changing your frequency, and you're changing your attractions.

Let's take a money example: when will I make money? When will I be rich? Check how you feel. You actually feel okay because this is a very okay question. Uncertain actually very confused, very lost. Now try this "Why do I always have the exact amount of money I always need?" "Why do I effortlessly have the exact amount of money I always need?" Now check how you feel. You feel blessed. Now here's another question: why am I attracting such big opportunities? Suddenly check how you feel. You suddenly feel awesome and blessed.

May I Ask You For a Small Favor?

I want to express my sincere gratitude for choosing to invest your time in reading this book. Your decision to explore this work among countless others means a lot to me.

I hope that within these pages, you've discovered actionable insights that can enhance your daily life. Your journey doesn't have to end here, though.

May I kindly request an additional 30 seconds of your valuable time?

Sharing your thoughts about the book through a review would be immensely appreciated. Your review serves as a beacon, guiding other readers to take a chance on my books. It's a small gesture that carries significant weight in the world of authors.

To submit your review effortlessly, please **Scan** the **QR Code** below. It will take you directly to the book's review page:

"The Power Of One Question"

Alternatively, you can also find the "**Reviews Section**" of this book's page on Amazon.

Your review will require just a minute of your time but will make a monumental difference in helping me connect with a broader audience and I eagerly look forward to reading your review.

Once again, thank you for your unwavering support of my work.

Chapter 6
The Influence of Questions on Relationships and Interactions

"The power of a single question can reshape your thinking, alter your actions, and define your legacy." – Sooraj Achar

So you need to choose what you want to feel and decide the questions based on that small specific question. There is another type of question which I will tell you. But first I would like all of you to take your notepads and recognize negative, small specific questions that you've been asking yourself for your HRCM, for your health, for your relationships, for your career, and for money. What are the small specific negative questions that you've been asking? Write down all the negative questions that you ask yourself during the day, this will help you to remember all your negatives so that you can work on them to fix them.

If you are married, do you ever ask your partner "Why don't you listen to me?" Almost every married couple has this problem. Do you want to hypnotize your partner to listen to you? I know you are getting excited. Go to your partner, look in your partner's eyes, and say, tell me one thing. Why are you such a good listener? You always listen to me so well. Why are you such a good listener? Ask this question to your partner three times a day. Look in their eyes and ask why you are such a good listener. Why are you so good at practicing the law of traction? Why are you so good at listening to all the lessons of the Law of Attraction? Check, how do you feel? You suddenly feel wonderful. Unfortunately, what we do is we ask people negative questions. So what do we extract from them? Negativity.

What you transmit to people is what you attract from people. For example, you may have seen radio walkie-talkies in movies. Policemen or military people used to communicate with each other; both walkie-talkies have two abilities. It has the ability to transmit. It also has the ability to attract from the other transmitter. So, both work as a transmitter and receiver. We as human beings are always doing transmission and attraction. If you transmit negative questions to other people, what will you attract from them? Negative answers from their subconscious. If you transmit a lot of positive questions to them, what will you attract from them? Positive attraction.

Many parents make the mistake of asking this question to their children. Why are you so lazy? Why don't you study on time? They ask small specific negative questions to children. Why don't you remember what you learned? Why don't you do your homework on time? Why don't you brush on time? Why don't you wear your coat properly? What are you doing? They are hypnotizing them with negative thoughts. And they are not just hypnotizing their children, they are hypnotizing themselves. They are hypnotizing their parents; they are hypnotizing their life partner. And they're programming everybody around them to give them more negativity. But if you change your transmission, you can change your attraction.

Let's take another example. Ask your child from now onwards; tell me why you remember things so easily? What have you done nowadays? Simply ask and see what happens. You're programming them by asking; suddenly you've become so good at studies nowadays. What happened? What have you done now? Will they really have an answer? No. But will they take the compliment? Yeah. So imagine you ask your child, you've become very hardworking nowadays, why is that? What have you done? Your child will many times say, I don't know. But they will get into their head. This is called Seeding. Seeding can be done in many ways.

But questioning is one of the most powerful ways. So, ask small specific questions. But first recognize what are the small specific negative questions that you're asking yourself, your relationships, your career, and your money on a daily basis. Because the more you can catch them, the more you can change them.

It would help if you first recognized your negative questions because the awareness of your negative questions is critical. If you don't do the diagnosis, the solution will not happen. Write down all your negative questions on a paper in one place so you're aware of them. Make good quality questions. Don't ask fake questions otherwise, your subconscious will not support you.

I'll tell you how to make it even more powerful by adding "I don't know why" in the beginning. For example: sometimes when we are sad, we should say- I don't know why I'm feeling sad. We have just reversed the question. "I don't know why my partner always listens to me" etc. When you add I don't know why, it makes it even easier for the subconscious mind. Can we add a negative to a negative statement? Why do I dislike junk food? Yeah, of course we can. This can be like: "I don't know why, I just don't like junk food". It's a very good question, it's a negative question. It helps your subconscious. "I don't know why I get so many jobs regularly" etc.

You're trying to hypnotize your life partner. Now you can try using it on your mother-in-law. It will work. Go to your mother and say, Mom, how come you are always on my side instead of your son's side? Why do you always do that? Now what is she going to say? No, I'm not on your side. No, she's not going to say that. But you've seated this thought in the subconscious like she's always on your side.

And all you had to do was change your specific question. This has to become a practice from today. Promise yourself that you will read these questions on a regular basis. But the idea here is that it's not a simple assignment of reading the questions. It's a practice of changing your questions regularly. Just keep changing your questions from negative to positive and you will start feeling your frequency changing.

That was one part. Now let's go to the second part.

Chapter 7

BIG LIFE QUESTIONS AND THEIR INFLUENCE ON YOUR LIFE

"A well-crafted question can be the compass guiding you towards the life you've always envisioned." – Sooraj Achar

Now we ask big life questions. The reason I call them big life questions is because these are questions that are big and they impact your entire life. They create frequency not only for one

THE POWER OF ONE QUESTION

area of your life but also for HRCM. For example, why am I not confident? Why am I so inferior? It's a big life question because it impacts all four areas. Why am I short-tempered? It's also a big question because you can be short-tempered in your health, relationship, career, and money everywhere. Like you can go to the gym and be angry. You can make money and be angry. So if you're simply asking yourself generic questions that impact all areas of your life, those are called big life questions. I'll tell you one of my examples of a big life question. This used to impact me a lot many, many years ago. And the question I used to ask myself is what's the point? I used to go for a holiday, I used to wait for a holiday, I used to be super excited for the holiday, I should prepare for the holiday, I used to wait one month desperately for the holiday, and then the day I would reach the holiday. I'll look everywhere and say, yeah, I've come, but what's the big deal? What's the point? This question is a life killer. It's a life experience killer. And the reason I call it a life killer is because it can lead people to depression. It can lead people to suicide.

Because they do anything in life. They do everything in life. And they ask like, what's the point? And it just drops your experience of everything. And just instantly imagine you desperately waiting for a holiday for one month. You reach there and after 2 hours you're like, I waited so much for this but what's the point? There's no big deal coming here. Everything is still the same. It drops your entire experience of life. If you keep asking what's the point of everything, are you going to be motivated or demotivated? You're going to be demotivated, right? People who are demotivated, people who are lazy keep asking this question all the time. They get a thought of exercising and they're like, what's the point? So they don't exercise. They try to think about marriage and say, let's find a life partner. And then their mind says but what's the point? It's okay. So then you don't like to find a life partner. You try to find a job. And even if I get a job, what's the point? People are still not going to call me successful. This is how we sabotage our own success. When your frequency is down, you get a higher opportunity but you sabotage yourself down. Sabotage means you self-destruct. You got something amazing, you made a silly mistake, and you sabotaged your own success. Why does that happen? Because your frequency is low. How do you change that? First recognize all your big life questions, which impact all areas of life.

An example of that in one of the earlier courses I remember, there was a lady who said, why am I so unlucky? Is this a small specific question or a big life question? Big life question. Like everywhere she was attracting bad luck, and wherever little bit she was attracting good luck, she had another question. Is this real? She had doubtful questions. And then some sabotage would happen, and she says, see, I told you I'm unlucky. And then she would again ask the question after sometimes saying: but why am I so unlucky? And then it used to go into a loop. She changed that question, and suddenly money started flowing in life, health started flowing in life, and relationships started flowing in life. Everything started going up. It's a matter of you changing your frequency with that one or two big life questions that you're asking yourself. But you don't always have one big life question. Sometimes you have multiple big life questions. For example, why am I not confident right now? Don't go into specifics right now. We've covered specific ones later in the chapter. Why am I not confident about making money? That is specific. But if you are saying, why am I not confident? That applies to every area of life. Most of us have two to three big life questions that impact our entire lives. Like, for me, one of the biggest questions was what's the point? And I'll tell you one of the people who will ask this question a lot. If you have a spiritual background, which means at a very early age, you were exposed to spirituality, you were exposed to religion, God, all those puja paths, and everything. So you'll see, spirituality fits in your head that even if you achieve a lot, there's no point. So you keep asking yourself, what's the point? And it kept self-destructing for a long period of time.

Chapter 8

Mastering Big Life Questions

"The secret of greatness often resides in the simplicity of one powerful question."
– Sooraj Achar

Now it's time to recognize your big life questions. So take your notepads, take a blank page, and write down all your big life negative questions that you've been asking yourself which impact all areas of life. You may have two to five such big questions that you keep asking yourself. And believe me; it's very easy to find this because you're using these questions every day. So think and write it down. What are the big life questions that you're using, which drop your frequency during the day?

Here are a few examples of Big Life Questions:

Why am I always so guilty?

Why don't I ever get what I deserve?

Why do I always get things with so much struggle?

Why is my life so difficult?

Why me always?

Why is this happening to me?

Why am I stuck?

Why do I make wrong decisions in life?

Why do I always have to fight for small things in life?

Why can't things change for the better?

Why am I not growing?

Why am I never able to close anything when I start?

THE POWER OF ONE QUESTION

All these questions have huge negative emotions. These are the questions that lead to depression. These are the questions that lead to panic attacks. These are the questions that lead to self-doubt, low self-esteem, and an inferiority complex. All those low frequencies. If you don't have these questions, you cannot have those low frequencies. So how do you change this? It doesn't take too much time. It's not rocket science. Take another two minutes. Convert all these questions into new questions. For example, why do I always have to be responsible? Let's change that. How come I always find people who support me? That's a good question. Specific question. But it's a good question related to responsibility.

Another one: Why am I nervous while speaking? We can change it to: Why am I so comfortable while speaking? Just change all your questions.

Another example: Why am I emotionally struggling? You can change it to: I don't know why I'm emotionally so stable. I don't know why people keep asking me why you're emotionally so stable. I don't know why. That's a big life question.

Now I hope you are done converting all your questions. Now think what did we do? What did we change? Just questions. Just some questions here and there. And our entire life has changed. Now, you cannot understand this me clarifying more. You can only understand this by practicing more. Once you get into the negative questions mode, you're always into like, how do I practice this? What does that mean? And the more you get into negative questions, the more your questions take you down. Whenever we are asking questions about the Law of Attraction, we're always asking negative questions in life. Like, why am I not attracting this? What is the affirmation for that? How do I do this? How do I do that? Constantly into negative questions. That's why they don't help. That's why I don't allow questions. Because what helps you is your practice, not your questions. And if you have to ask questions, what kind of questions will you ask? Negative questions or positive questions? Simple.

So to give you an answer to my question that I used to ask earlier, which is what's the point? I converted it into a very simple question. How can I appreciate what I have right now? How can I really be grateful for what I have right now? So an example: when I used to go on holidays earlier, my question was, what's the point? Now when I go on holiday, I say, okay, so I'm here. How can I appreciate this holiday? How can I be grateful for this holiday? How can I enjoy this holiday more? The more I ask, how can I appreciate this more? How can I be grateful for this more? How can I enjoy this more? Automatically my frequency is shifting.

Instead of asking 'Why am I alive?' How about asking wow, what am I going to do with this beautiful life? That's a much better question. So what do we do from now onwards? Take control of the one person's questions in the world that controls you, who's that one person? You.

Chapter 9

TAKING CONTROL OF YOUR FREQUENCY

"In the grand story of your life, every chapter begins with a single question." –
Sooraj Achar

Now the second thing I'd like you to be careful about people in your life, they are going to ask you questions consciously. They ask you negative questions to program your subconscious mind. You don't know they're doing it. They don't know they're doing it. But they're doing it just like you ask your children, why are you lazy? So people will ask you, why don't you listen to me? Instead of getting carried away by them and getting irritated, ask a question back. But what question would you ask? A positive question or a negative question? Here is an example: If I ask you, why don't you listen to me? Think about what positive question can you throw back at me instead of getting irritated with my question quickly. You should answer like this: Oh, I don't okay. How would you like me to listen to you? Here's another one: What can I do to listen to you more effectively? What can I do to convince you that I care? The more you're asking questions that are positive you are changing not just your frequency, you're changing. Their frequency also.

Let me give you one last example: we all have two frequencies within us. What are those two frequencies? Positive frequency and negative frequency. The person with the Majority Frequency will dominate the other. Let me explain if my Frequency is more positive, and if your frequency is negative but less negative but my Positivity is bigger than your negativity, I will impact you. Similarly, if your negativity is bigger than my Positivity, you will impact me because I'm allowing that. I'll give you a very simple example: There is vanilla ice cream and there's some chocolate sauce on the ice cream. Which will dominate in taste? If you eat that ice cream what will you taste more, vanilla or chocolate? Of course, Vanilla because the vanilla is dominating the chocolate. Because the chocolate is less in quantity. Similarly, if you take your vanilla again pour a mug full of chocolate sauce on it. Now what will you taste? Only chocolate. The vanilla disappears. Whoever has the majority frequency will always attract and will always get influenced, and will always dominate. So if you have someone else who's giving you negative frequency, they're transmitting negativity to you. I'm not saying no, but the reason you're getting impacted is because you are less positive. So they will dominate you. But let's say they're giving me a lot of negativity and I have more positivity. Now who will impact whom? Now we will impact them. So don't complain about why people are negative. The question you have to

THE POWER OF ONE QUESTION

ask is, how can I increase my Positivity? Like, people keep asking me this question: how can I handle toxic people? And the question I ask them is, how can you become more and more positive? That's a more important question. Rather than asking how I can handle toxic people? Because if you are more positive and if toxic people come close to you, you know what will happen? Their toxicity will convert into positivity and they will become more positive.

You may have heard about this beautiful story of the person who wrote Ramayana, we all know Walmiki. Who was Walmiki? Was he a positive person? No, he was a negative person. He was a thief. But the more he started reading Ramayana, he became Ram. The Positivity of Ramayana converted a thief into a good human being. This was possible with all of us. Are you going to be impacted by other people's negativity? Or are you going to impact other people by your Positivity? What are you going to do? So from today onwards, instead of asking the question, how do I handle negative people? What do you have to ask? How do I become more positive? The answer is simple. Ask more powerful, beautiful questions. So from now onwards, make your Positivity bigger than other people's negativity.

Now, how can we use this to handle conflict management? I'll tell you how. Somebody is angry with you. Instead of asking why these people don't listen to me, here's another question. Why am I so good at influencing people? Why am I so good at convincing people? Why am I so good at selling? I ask this question to myself many, many times. My question is why am I so good at negotiations? And believe me, over a period of time I became very good at negotiations. Instead of asking why me? Ask yourself, why not me? Like for example, would you like your neighbors to go through your problems? Do you want to take your problems and give them to the neighbor? Let's say your neighbor has a small child. You want to take all your problems and give them to the neighbor's child, No. So who would you like to give? Do you want all your problems to be experienced by me? Who do you want to give all these problems to? Nobody. So then the question shouldn't be Why me? The question shouldn't be Why not me? Somebody gives you more responsibility saying instead of asking Why me?

Chapter 10

The Art of Question Mastery for Self-Improvement

"The power of one question lies in the limitless possibilities it holds." – Sooraj Achar

Assignment Number One:

This assignment is very critical. You must recognize as many negative questions as you can of your big life questions and your small specific questions. Is it 100% necessary to categorize them this way? No, not necessary. It helps if you can, but it's not necessary. Is it possible that you will make the mistake of having a big life question categorized as small? And is it possible that you might make the mistake of making a small as a big question? That's okay if you categorize wrong. The category is not so important. The only important part is to recognize what are the negative questions you're asking in your life. And then the second part of the exercise is very critical. You must change all your big life questions which are negative and all your small life small specific questions which are negative into positive and powerful questions. That's your assignment number- one.

Assignment Number Two:

Look at these new questions along with the old questions. So we can see the comparison. Like what my old question was and what my new question is. By comparing these questions you will be activating your subconscious mind, you are telling your mind that you are fixing your mistakes, you are changing yourself, you are updating to the best. I know it's a little bit of homework but we have to do it if we want the change. It'll not just help you; it'll help many other people.

Assignment Number Three:

Repeat your positive questions again and again. But the condition is not in your mind. How will you repeat your question? Repeat them loudly. Stand up in front of a mirror so that you can observe yourself getting energized and start repeating the positive questions loudly. Your big life questions, your small specific questions again and again. Do this multiple times a day. Feel the energy, feel the magic happening, feel the things changing around you, feel people changing around, and feel yourself changing day by day.

CONCLUSION

Congratulations on reaching the culmination of this book. Your commitment to reading through these pages signifies your dedication to personal growth and a thirst for knowledge. Completing a book is a remarkable achievement, and you should take a moment to acknowledge your accomplishment.

Throughout this journey, the aim has been to guide you toward shaping a destiny defined by success and fulfillment. Your investment in this book reflects a deep commitment to self-improvement, and for that, you should feel proud.

As you conclude this book, I trust that it has left you with valuable insights and a sense of empowerment. The road to a prosperous destiny is not always linear or without its challenges, but your newfound knowledge in smart questioning equips you to navigate these paths with confidence. I genuinely hope that your voyage through these chapters has been both enlightening and engaging. The pursuit of a splendid life brimming with happiness and fulfillment is a commendable one, and your proactive steps toward this aspiration are evident through your persistence in reading this book.

In the pursuit of success and a life well-lived, remember that knowledge is your most potent tool. With this, you hold the key to unlocking the limitless potential within you. As you close this final page and embark on the journey that follows, I extend my heartfelt best wishes for a future filled with accomplishments and contentment.

Cheers,
Sooraj Achar

MAY I ASK YOU FOR A SMALL FAVOR?

I want to express my sincere gratitude for choosing to invest your time in reading this book. Your decision to explore this work among countless others means a lot to me.

I hope that within these pages, you've discovered actionable insights that can enhance your daily life. Your journey doesn't have to end here, though.

May I kindly request an additional 30 seconds of your valuable time?

Sharing your thoughts about the book through a review would be immensely appreciated. Your review serves as a beacon, guiding other readers to take a chance on my books. It's a small gesture that carries significant weight in the world of authors.

To submit your review effortlessly, please **Scan the QR Code** below. It will take you directly to the book's review page:

"The Power Of One Question"

Alternatively, you can also find the "**Reviews Section**" of this book's page on Amazon.

Your review will require just a minute of your time but will make a monumental difference in helping me connect with a broader audience and I eagerly look forward to reading your review.

Once again, thank you for your unwavering support of my work.

PREVIEW OF MY BEST SELLING BOOKS

Numerology Mastery Series

★ **Why do 80% of People Fail to Recognize their True Potential ??**

This **Self-Help** book will help you **Recognize, Transform and Navigate** your life toward a **Happier Destiny**.

I always say that your **Date of Birth** is so precious. God has placed many diamonds on your date of birth you are not aware of. It doesn't matter if your date of birth is good or bad. The idea is how you can take the best out of your date of birth. **Master Your DESTINY With Numerology** is a perfect,

complete beginner's guide for those who are new to numerology.

★ What Role Does Numerology Play in Your Life?

- You have been surrounded by numbers since the day you were Born. Now use them to unlock your Destiny.

- Wherever you go in your life, the numbers always move on with you.

- When you are born, on the very first day of your life, you get your date of birth, which is made up of numbers.

- When you get admitted to school, you get your roll number.

- When you get your results, you get a percentage of numbers.

- When you get a job, you get a salary and EMP-ID number.

- When you buy any vehicle, it has a number plate.

- When you travel, you get a ticket and seat number

- When you check into a hotel, you get a room number.

- When you want to call a person, you have to dial numbers.

- When you get married, there is also a date attached to it.

- If there is Life, there are Numbers. You cannot get rid of Numbers.

★ Your **Name Spelling** also plays an important role according to your date of birth. Believe me or not, **30% to 40%** of your success or failure depends on your name spelling. If you keep your name spelling correct, you can achieve 30% to 40% more success in your life.

♥ Master Your DESTINY With Numerology will help you...

✓ Recognize Your Strengths and Weaknesses.

✓ Find Your Lucky Numbers and Colors.

✓ Correct Your Name Spelling without changing your documents.

✓ Choose the Right Profession.

✓ Find a Compatible Life-Partner.

✓ With Simple Remedies for All Your Problems.

✓ Check Your Foreign or Abroad Opportunities.

✓ Predict your Future Years, Months, and Days of importance, which helps you take Better Decisions.

✓ Understand the Behavioral Patterns of People Around You.

✓ Transform and Navigate your life for a Better Future.

★ If you are ready to make a commitment to yourself that you want to learn everything that is presented to you, then it is our commitment to you that this will surely help you a lot. There is no reason why this book will not change your destiny or transform your future. But, there is an important thing you must keep in mind, i.e., **"You will bring this change through TRANSFORMATION, not through MIRACLES"**.

★ If you learn **Numerology**, then

(a) "You will be **awakened**", which makes it likely to "**transform**" your life.

(b) Ultimately, "You will be able to **navigate** your life".

★ Life is all about "**Awakening**,", "**Transformation**," and eventually, "Knowing How To **Navigate** It?"

★ Order **Master Your DESTINY With Numerology** now to make the most of your

Health, Relationships, Career, and Money by unlocking the **Power of Numbers**.

Check Out My Best Selling Books Here

Numerology Mastery Series

1. Master Your DESTINY With Numerology

2. Master Your NAME-SPELLING With Numerology

3. Master Your RELATIONSHIPS With Numerology

4. Master Your GOALS With Numerology

Vastu Mastery Series

★ How Can These Books Work Miracles in Your Life?

This Self-Help Book is A Perfect Blueprint Describing Ancient Principles for Modern Living. A Step-by-step Practical Guide for Beginners to Creating a Positive Living Space and for Optimal Well-Being.

Learn:

★ How to Implement Feng-Shui/Vastu in your Day-to-Day Life !!

★ What Role Do Feng-Shui and Vastu Play in Your Life?

★ Relationship between Vastu and Feng-Shui?

Vastu is used to Diagnose, and Feng Shui is the Remedy. Vastu is used to identify the disease, and Feng Shui is the medicine. Vastu and Feng Shui are complementary to each other.

Vastu Shastra is an Ancient Indian Science of architecture and construction, which is based on the principles of harmony and balance between humans and their environment. The main focus of Vastu is to create a harmonious balance between the 5-Elements of nature, i.e., Earth, Water, Air, Fire, & Space. It emphasizes directions and orientation and uses various elements like colors, shapes, and materials to create a balance and positive energy in the living spaces.

Feng Shui, on the other hand, is a Chinese Philosophical System of harmonizing everyone with the surrounding environment. It is based on the principles of Qi (Chi), the life force that flows through all living things, and Yin and Yang, the balance of opposite forces. Feng Shui focuses on the placement of objects, furniture, and structures in living spaces to optimize the flow of energy, or "Qi." It also considers the orientation of the building, the placement of doors and windows, and the use of colors, shapes, & materials to create balance & harmony.

In summary, both Vastu and Feng Shui aim to create balance and harmony in living spaces, but Vastu is more focused on directions and orientation, while Feng Shui emphasizes the flow of energy & balance of opposing forces.

★ The Benefits of Reading This Book Include:

✓ **Health and Well-Being:** Vastu principles aim to create a harmonious and balanced environment that can promote physical, mental, and emotional well-being.

✓ **Financial Prosperity:** Vastu principles are believed to help attract positive energy and good fortune, leading to financial prosperity.

✓ **Improved Relationships:** Vastu principles can help create an atmosphere of peace and harmony, which can lead to improved relationships with family, friends, & colleagues.

✓ **Increased Productivity:** A Vastu-compliant environment is said to be conducive to productivity and efficiency, leading to greater success in personal & professional life.

✓ **Spiritual Growth:** Vastu principles are based on ancient Vedic knowledge and aim to promote spiritual growth & enlightenment.

✓ **Enhanced Creativity:** Vastu principles are believed to enhance creativity and inspiration, which can be beneficial for artists, writers, & other creative professionals.

✓ **Better Sleep Quality:** Vastu principles can help create a peaceful and relaxing environment, which can improve the quality of sleep and help reduce stress & anxiety.

✓ **Improved Mental Clarity:** A Vastu-compliant environment is said to help clear the mind and improve mental clarity, which can be beneficial for decision-making & problem-solving.

✓ **Enhanced Career Prospects:** Vastu principles can help align one's career goals with their personal strengths and abilities, leading to greater career success & satisfaction.

★ Overall, the benefits of Vastu can contribute to a more Balanced, Harmonious, & Fulfilling Life.

★ Order "Master Your DESTINY With Vastu" now to make the most of your Health, Relationships, Career, & Money by unlocking the Power of Directions.

Check Out My Best Selling Books Here

1. Master Your DESTINY With Vastu

2. Master Your GROWTH With Vastu

3. Master Your WEALTH With Vastu

4. Master Your CAREER With Vastu

The Ultimate Self-Healing Mastery Series

"The Art of Balancing Yin-Yang Energy" is an enlightening and transformative guide that unveils the ancient wisdom of harmonizing the opposing forces of Yin and Yang within ourselves and the world around us. Drawing from the profound teachings of Eastern philosophy and modern-day practices, this book offers a comprehensive understanding of Yin and Yang and provides practical techniques to achieve balance, harmony, and fulfillment in all aspects of life.

In today's fast-paced and chaotic world, finding balance is more crucial than ever. Whether you seek to improve your relationships, enhance your well-being, or achieve success in your career, understanding and aligning the Yin-Yang energy within you can be a game-changer. This book takes you on a transformative journey, guiding you through the principles, practices, and benefits of embracing the art of balancing Yin-Yang energy.

By delving into the core concepts of Yin and Yang, you will gain insights into their dynamic interplay and learn how to identify and rectify imbalances in your life. Discover how the complementary forces of Yin and Yang manifest in various aspects, such as work-life balance, emotional well-being, and personal growth. With this knowledge, you can cultivate harmony and create a fulfilling and purpose-driven life.

★ Here are the <u>Top-15 Benefits:</u>

1. Harmony and Balance: Balancing yin-yang energy promotes a sense of harmony and balance within oneself and in relationships with others.

2. Enhanced Well-being: Balanced yin-yang energy contributes to overall physical, mental, and emotional well-being.

3. Stress Reduction: Maintaining balanced yin-yang energy helps reduce stress and promotes a state of calmness and relaxation.

4. Increased Energy: Balancing yin-yang energy enhances vitality and boosts energy levels.

5. Emotional Stability: Harmonizing yin-yang energy supports emotional stability, reducing mood swings and promoting emotional resilience.

6. Improved Focus and Clarity: Balanced yin-yang energy enhances mental clarity, concentration, and focus.

7. Better Decision-Making: When yin-yang energy is in equilibrium, it fosters better decision-making skills and promotes sound judgment.

8. Enhanced Intuition: Balancing yin-yang energy can amplify intuition and inner wisdom.

9. Improved Relationships: Harmonizing yin-yang energy cultivates healthier and more balanced relationships, promoting understanding and cooperation.

10. Greater Creativity: Balanced yin-yang energy can enhance creativity and innovation in various aspects of life.

11. Physical Healing: Balancing yin-yang energy supports the body's natural healing abilities and can contribute to faster recovery from illnesses or injuries.

12. Emotional Healing: Harmonizing yin-yang energy aids in emotional healing and facilitates the release of emotional blockages.

13. Enhanced Digestion: Balanced yin-yang energy promotes optimal digestion and helps alleviate digestive issues.

14. Hormonal Balance: Balancing yin-yang energy can help regulate hormonal imbalances and improve overall hormonal health.

15. Improved Sleep Quality: Harmonized yin-yang energy promotes better sleep quality and can help alleviate sleep disorders.

Check Out My Best Selling Books Here

 **1. The Art of Balancing YIN-YANG Energy**

 **2. The 7 Energy Needs**

 **3. The Fear of Death**

 **4. The Power of One Question**

TESTIMONIALS

These are a few feedbacks from my clients across different parts of the world. Kindly go through their reviews to understand how Numerology and Vastu helped them.

1. Ekta Gupta – Kolkata, India

> *"2021 is a difficult year for me. I have consulted a few numerologists. I have received vague answers and complicated solutions. I'm new to numerology. Charges were expensive. Sooraj is a good and kind soul. He is very patient with me. He answered all my questions. I had 1000 questions. More ever he helped me*

to find a business name with no extra charges. I'm grateful to him. With your help, I'm sorted out with my business name. I had a lot of anxiety about it. I'm confident now. Sooraj is a helpful soul. He is patient and explains if one has questions. He doesn't rush into closing the job. You can consult him easily. I am going to recommend him to newbies like me. He is not going to cheat you or misguide you".

2. Neetu Ganglani - Stanley, Hongkong

"Hello Sooraj, I can't thank you enough. At the age of 45, I could find an ideal life partner for myself. And my compatibility with the boy I like. Got to know our strengths and weaknesses. Your suggestions helped me to find the right life partner. You have a bright future. Good luck"

3. Lensly Kwaimani - Solomon Islands, Oceania

"Dear friend, glad I came across you. My daughter Felinda Kwaimani is sick for a long time and I was very much worried. Thank you for giving suggestions and guidance".

4. Seham Shabhir - Talagang, Pakistan

"You're one of the best numerologists...your predictions are correct...you are a very humble person...you gave answers to all of my questions in detail ... I'm very thankful to you. Ur remedies prove very helpful for me. He is the very best numerologist... I recommend him for all.. u should consult him to get rid of your problems..his remedies work like a magic"

5. Naveen Kumar - Bengaluru, India

"Sooraj is a gem as a human and as a professional. Before approaching Sooraj, I have enquired and got inputs from other numerologists and I did some research as well. I Was not satisfied with the answers provided by them and most of them were behind fees, even after paying for the consultation they charge extra for clarifying doubts. However, Sooraj was awesome in client satisfaction and the way he follows up with the client for providing suggestions. He takes the initiative to follow up and provide the best solutions and describes the reason for the input. I definitely suggest Sooraj to anyone who is looking for start-up business names or anything related to numerology. He has a good amount of knowledge and patience to answer all my queries".

6. Sneha S - Karnataka, India

"Hi Sooraj, it's a great prediction starting from Personality Traits to our Abroad Opportunities to future achievements. Everything is perfectly predicted with correct proof and explanations which help us to understand our lives better and take steps accordingly to numerology. Everyone are curious to know more about their life just to know when, how & what situations they will come across and how they need to overcome everything. Thanks a lot, Sooraj, for the best Numerology Prediction which helped us to understand ourselves better".

7. Aditya S - Mumbai, India

"Sooraj, your numerology predictions are brilliant and accurate. Your Suggestions

helped me find out whether my current job is suitable for me or not. I would suggest people consult you in due course of time".

8. Nabanita M - West Bengal, India

"Hi Sooraj, it's helpful and gives me a quick idea and help. Thank you so much for being there. It helped me to understand my situation It helps in my career and marriage. The information is good".

9. Naresh – Bangalore, India

"Hello Sooraj, it was satisfactory. Can decide further based on the info shared & also can see positive outcomes looking forward to checking how it works".

10. Harishchandra Dnyaneshwar Deshmukh – Delhi, India

"Hi sir, Padhai puri nahi kar paya, 11 k salary he, Stable nahi hu life me, Business success nahi milta. Thank u sir for sharing my report and helping me understand my strengths and weaknesses".

AUTHOR PROFILE

 Follow **the Author's Profile Page** to get updates on all his books : **https://amazon.com/author/sooraj_achar**

 Grab your **Free Gift** if you missed it: **https://gift.sooraj-achar.com/**

 Please Leave Your **Valuable Review** here: **"The Power of One Question"**

 For 1-to-1 consultation, scan the **QR code** or contact: **connect@sooraj-achar.com**

 Follow the **Author's BookBub** Profile:

https://www.bookbub.com/authors/sooraj-achar

Stay Connected to the **Author's Social Media Handles** below:

https://amzn.to/3CgQHF9

https://medium.com/@soorajachar99

https://bit.ly/3M7gIu2

instagram.com/psychology_of_numberz/

https://bit.ly/3dO6aDh

https://bit.ly/3LXBTyz

https://bit.ly/3E9vKxc

DISCLAIMER

This book is for educational purposes only. Readers acknowledge that the author does not render legal, financial, medical, or professional advice. The content within this book has been derived from various sources. Please consult a licensed professional before attempting any techniques outlined in this book.

By reading this document, the reader agrees that under no circumstances is the author responsible for any direct or indirect losses incurred as a result of the use of the information contained within this document, including but not limited to errors, omissions, or inaccuracies.

Adherence to all applicable laws and regulations, including international, federal, state, and local governing professional licensing, business practices, advertising, and all other jurisdictions, is the sole responsibility of the purchaser or reader.

Neither the author nor the publisher assumes any responsibility or liability whatsoever on behalf of the purchaser or reader of these materials. Any perceived slight of any individual or organization is purely unintentional.

Printed in Great Britain
by Amazon